Published in Great Britain in 2014 by Canongate Books Ltd,
14 High Street, Edinburgh EH1 1TE

canongate.co.uk

7

British Library Cataloguing-in-Publication Data
A catalogue record for this book is available on
request from the British Library

ISBN 978 1 78211 113 9

PEANUTS written and drawn by Charles M. Schulz
Edited by Andy Miller and Jenny Lord
Design: Rafaela Romaya
Layout: Stuart Polson

CHARLES M. SCHULZ

THE PHILOSOPHY OF
SNOOPY

CANONGATE

I SHOULD THINK YOU'D GET BORED JUST SITTING ON A DOGHOUSE ALL DAY..

ON THE CONTRARY..

WHO COULD GET BORED FLYING THE STAR SHIP "ENTERPRISE"?

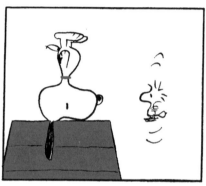

Dear Contributor,
We regret to inform you that your manuscript does not suit our present needs. The Editors

BAM!

CRASH

STOMP! STOMP!
STOMP! STOMP!

P.S. Don't take it out on your mailbox.

IF YOU THINK ABOUT SOMETHING AT THREE O'CLOCK IN THE MORNING AND THEN AGAIN AT NOON THE NEXT DAY, YOU GET DIFFERENT ANSWERS..

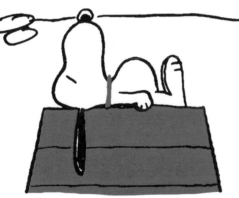